# NOT
# YOUR
# MAMA'S
# MELTING
# POT

D1606642

# NOT
# YOUR
# MAMA'S
# MELTING
# POT

Poems

Benjamín Naka-Hasebe Kingsley

*2017 Backwaters Prize Winner*
Bob Hicok, Judge

The Backwaters Press

The Backwaters Press
1124 Pacific St., #8392
Omaha, NE, 68108
(402) 451-4052
www.thebackwaterspress.com

The Backwaters Press

Published 2018 by The Backwaters Press

Kingsley, Benjamín Naka-Hasebe
    Not Your Mama's Melting Pot / Benjamín Naka-Hasebe Kingsley.
    ISBN-10: 1-935218-49-2
    ISBN-13: 978-1-935218-49-4 (pb)
    Library of Congress Control Number: 2018938434

Front cover artwork: *Reliquary 1* © 2016 by Cannupa Hanska
Cover design, interior design, and typesetting by Zach Marell
The text of this book is set in Adobe Garamond Pro.

*First Edition*

Printed in the United States of America

For the Clan Mothers

For the Fire Keepers

For John

*That's the thing about the American Dream…*
*you have to be asleep to believe it.*

— George Carlin

# Acknowledgements

Un fuerte abrazo to the journals and anthologies in which many of these poems appeared, sometimes in earlier forms:

*Best New Poets 2017* (ed. Natalie Diaz)
*Proud to Be: Writing by American Warriors, Volume 6*
*Tupelo Press Native Voices: Honoring Indigenous Poetry*

*Akitsu Quarterly*
*American Indian Culture and Research Journal*
*Cincinnati Review*
*Colorado Review*
*Crab Orchard Review*
*Deep Water Literary Journal*
*diode poetry journal*
*International Journal of Indigenous Literature*
*The Iowa Review*
*Little Patuxent Review*
*The Massachusetts Review*
*the minnesota review*
*Missouri Review*
*Narrative Magazine*
*New American Writing*
*Ninth Letter*
*Oxford Poetry*
*PANK Magazine*
*PEN America*
*The Poetry Review*
*Poetry Swindon*
*Prairie Schooner*
*Puerto del Sol*
*Review Americana*
*The Southern Collective*
*Sugar House Review*
*Tin House*
*Typehouse Literary Magazine*
*Water-Stone Review*
*Waxwing*
*West Branch*

# Contents

The Hapa Anthem    5

—

"Pick your switch"    11

Jesus in a Jar of Mayonnaise    12

How I Learned to Climb Trees    13

"Buckshot Mouthwash"    15

When the Last Bricklayer Has Left    17

The Damned: Our Blue Yodel No. 9    20

Teach Me How to Deregulate Rage    22

0 to 60—One Horse in a Field    24

Escaping Carlisle Indian Industrial School    27

Tadodaho, Keeper of the People's History, of the Council Fire    29

Redeployment: Operation Noble Eagle, 14 September 2001—
    Present    31

Holler.    33

—

Warrior of The Rising Sun (1893-1959)    39

Obon, Festival of the Dead    42

Godzilla! vs. Six Links Trailer Park, an Unending Series of Tanka    45

Beneath Carnival Lights    48

Our Last WWF SummerSlam    50

The Down Syndrome Brother    52

At the End of My Street Corner: Jamaica, Queens    54

for a good boy we'll break all the rules    57

Misogi, the Patterned Act of Repenting    60

notes grandpa gave the search party upon his rescue    62

A Haibun to Define Kintsukuroi    64

—

Selling Cigars on a Coral Gables Corner 1987    69

Into the Red Devil's Horn    72

Contagion   75

The Beginning of Science Fiction   77

Light Escapes Us   79

When One Has Lived a Long Time Alone   81

Don't Speak   82

Mother Walks Free Despite Admitting Homicide in Daughter's Death
    on Tribal Lands   83

Teach a Man Cruelty and He'll Never Forget Your Face   85

So Much Depends   87

Loss of a Man's Tail: Baring One Native Son Bald   88

Los Alamos, New Mexico: An Open Letter to Radiation
    Poisoning   90

The Act of Soul Ferrying   92

Economy   96

Of Reach   97

"please take a seat, the doctor will see you shortly"   99

I Am   101


Notes   103

# NOT
# YOUR
# MAMA'S
# MELTING
# POT

## Artist Cannupa Hanska Luger on his cover art:

Reliquary; A container or shrine in which (a sacred object esteemed and venerated because of association with a saint or martyr, a survivor or remnant left after decay, disintegration, or disappearance, a trace of some past or outmoded practice, custom, or belief) are kept.

This body of work is a site-specific installation; where it would be shown influenced what would be shown. The display case is as much the piece as the actual objects. Behind glass any object is idolized. The object becomes a trophy, a symbol of the acclaim of the person or institution that houses it.

Ceramic animal skulls in a state of suspended decay portrayed by a variety of fibers are the relics. Hanging from the artificial gore is a ceramic knife. The knife is an icon of human interaction. This interaction supplies the viewer with responsibility, giving the object the esteem of martyr. It has died and we are to blame. The animal has perished for us, by us.

# The Hapa Anthem

*I move with the elegance of an African elephant.*
　　　　—"Banana Clipper," by Killer Mike and Run the Jewels

Badass top feeders. Real North Philly
boys.
　　　We were a tribe of concrete Natives
pigeon feathered　　　Latino Whiteys
Burnt Rice not wannabes:

　　*block boy skid stains　&　hijos of scarecrows*

they called us　　　brown

enough to smear an imagined girlfriend
　　& her white panties. "The Christo
Rey Sharks"　　　we monikered ourselves.
As if we wanted to run
　　far away but not yet forget our mother's—Christ,

　　we wanted to be Papi Chulos, we wanted to kaboom
　　(not bloom) into their language of how to make a home

　　　　　of dimpled hipbones. We supplicants eager
for tales of human humidors　　　filtered
through mocha cigars
　　& the sheen of yellow teeth
　　smoking on & on about the rudder of their tongues.

So we bowed
our mohawks our buzz cuts our sick fades
& we prayed

for jewels: encrusted fingers cresting
        ten-ringed & gold our necks thick


we bound our own feet
            with colorful shoelaces
like the lashings of a newborn
    kite soaring high above the Schuylkill


          we dangled from our bronzed Achilles.

Our spindly limbs unwound with age, & again we prayed
     for stereo systems     loud
             enough to outrun cop sirens
    hatcheting their red
       whites & past our saggy blue
           jeans     past our sandwiched crust
of uncut curb & we beat
    the tar across
    each other's faces & gleaming       bone-shot
we came into
    our own heart's leaking.
          Gaggles of fists we circled up
        in that apartment complex basement
        or this moon-gilded lot


empty.


& we spun each other's heads like well-oiled weathervanes.


We taught ourselves
    lessons we would be learning decades after

each decanting

        finding ourselves

unable to lift & light

    the wet firewood of our arms

& find the actuation to pray again

for
fingers
reaching
just above the parapet.

## "Pick your switch"

says my father        and I'm stepping

out into the backyard forest        the sycamores

are not a spilled latticework        of bent elbows not

the boney helter-skelter        cage of likely-beaten

boys they are just        fucking

trees.        I root

through God's        mottling

underbelly His surfacing        grasshopper lesions

root out a stick        who will come alive for me

like a snake        and when presented

to my father will coil        around the charred bark

of his forearm        bodied tight hinges of scales

and do the frenzied beating        of my heart

make my father's fist        turn

in on itself        like a Christmas ornament

like Moses's magic staff never        dreamt it could.

# Jesus in a Jar of Mayonnaise

"Why
they call it *Miracle    Whip*"     my daughter
age four    chops her hands
she a real know-it-all
like she's fixing   to put       this motherless kitchen
back in order

"Why
don't you watch me
turn this Whip   into wine"    I'll say
anything gets       her smiling

"Like Jesus?" my daughter
inhales         as if she just found sanctification
at the bottom          of this conversation's cereal box

*You think Jesus in that jar of mayonnaise?*

My mother said God ain't     have no white                man's face
but I still picture him white as mayonnaise     some fool
lifting him up        that sour wine       that vinegary sponge
on a tree branch sayin'    "here boy              drink"

So that night I pick up      Nutella for supper
we spread it around real   thick    our ham
cheese sandwiches     proper
dripping  No    substitutionary soybean oil     egg    vinegar water

*Nutella is a miracle*    says my daughter

"Yea mama" I say back

# How I Learned to Climb Trees

*from the language of the Onondaga Nation in outer Appalachia*

Hode'noda'. "Sing!" Say it out loud. Don't leave
our Res(ervations) behind or you'll die. Burnt paper skin,
the hocking sound at the back of his throat, they say
he ate like a wolf and slept like a bear. Scullery
of ribcage rising in the open air. I have done everything
but speak my own name, slurping on hands and knees
at the lip of white bucket in the room's bulging middle.
Outside, purple blossoms call to me. I think I want to strip
them like a shish kabob, let their meaty hearts bleed
across the three-leaf clover of my tongue. I rattle
broken deer antlers like drumsticks. I've skinned
frogs. I've been a real bastard. It's like
when he let me rub the divot, our
elbows entwined, so I'd be infested with the same
family of chiggers. So we could be koda. Brothers.
Be blessed by the red welts itching through
the tanned hide of our arm in arm. So a sometime-
father would pry into my wounds
with the slender coals of tweezer blades, squeezing
the heads of burrowed insects from my flesh. So I could feel
fingerprints seal closed the openness.
When my arm falls asleep at night, I think of koda. Brother. The alien
appendage attached to my corpse, making itself knowable.
Dream chiggers wake, alive, and skitter through the upper mantle
of my arm. Do we wake in rhythm? Does he dream of me
with a sideways mouth, poured from a cup of slender nose? I've heard
of how I used to stand in front of closed doors, calling his
name as if in a dream he was just beyond and I can hear

his necklace of rattling beads, smell the bonfire burning
of his armpits. I learned to walk in my sleep they say. I learned
to talk in my dreams. If I step through a door, I want to know
I will not fall through tree branches to the forest floor.
Where they found him. I must have seen him, bent over
that ancient log, he with an unzipped consciousness. Spilled. How old
was I? Three. Singing for the first time deeper and deeper
into the forest: *do la mi do la mi.* I'd lost
my voice by the time they found me.

## "Buckshot Mouthwash"

Wynona calls it cradling        a 20-gauge

& cracking open       its break-action

over her pregnant belly      thumbing two

red shells over       & under & grinning

peak      of her smile wider

than the summit      of Sugarloaf Knob

of this Appalachian foothill.      But damn

even with babies      sweltering inside

she can bushwhack      faster than a new car

through a Nickajack      so all us guys give

her a break about      coming rattlesnake

hunting out      of season in jean shorts.

Chet obliterates      a rattler's arrowed dome

concussive force      whipping its pale underbelly

kite string quick      cloud bound and raining blood.

I remember myself      now mouthful

of semi-straight teeth         instead of buckshot

in quiet eros       on that red evening how I

plucked the snake       her still strong & winding

around my forearm      a brilliance of scales

green black green      I knew she had wanted to live

not headless      not embarrassed into

a baby's first      rattle.

# When the Last Bricklayer Has Left

*Were the tower of my Father*
  *laid down over the plain*
*of Indiana, Pennsylvania, it would be*
  *a two-day journey to walk*
*from toenail to collarbone.*

            The crust of our front lawn gives
                  as my father winds upward in dusty paths
            so high I imagine the top of him must bend
                  so as not to scrape the ceiling of heaven.

Women and men have come with pickaxe
      trowel and carts of brick adding

to the height of my father. Generations pilgrimage
      along the near-infinite stretch of his soles. Burned

their fingers raw on the stitching of his sneakers. Oracled
      their futures through windows of rusted eyelets.

Rubbed clean the patina of his heels
      by the callous of their hooks. Lost themselves

in curled forests of black hair lacing each
      boney ankle. In my father, merchants' caravans

mill men and masons have fought for days
      to scale the smokestacks of his chins. Of death

I have heard the foreman shout down
      to his firstborn, watched the finality of sons falling

at my father's feet. Witnessed purpling necks sway
        limp from my father's shoelaces. Wind

claps an ocean of copper ingots turning over
        as a furnace in my father's pockets. Impenetrable.

Tilt your head back far as it will go and you can see
        black against the sun, squints of birds

shimmering along the muntin of my father's
        clavicles, sun peeling back sheets of snow

pleating skin over and again histories
        are sunken into folds of my father's flesh, unchartable

they say once you sail across the clay waves
        of his mane the sights are unspeakable. Structures

once stood around us erect as kilns
        fired mortars: brass cannonballs and bitumen jets

were nothing but pebbles in a boy's slingshot
        arcing across the bow of his DIXIE belt buckle.

But now the tower of his body is wholly unpeopled, the kilns
        at his feet unfired coals and my father ebbs so

old with spikes of newborn bird cherry and the many mouths
        of weeds. He is old and there is no other age

soon he will breach the ceiling
        of heaven and the length of him

I will climb as the last pilgrim past his left ear
and finally know him face to flickering eye.

# The Damned: Our Blue Yodel No. 9

*It's a long, long lane / that has no turning*
*It's a fire / that always keeps on burning*
*Sure as you were born / to die.*
        —Bessie Smith

It's just another requiem for Ragtown Ragers
where we're all sons & sometimes-daughters

of part-time Baptist preachers. Our nightly high
hyphenated by Bobby Belché backing

his pickup too damn far up & onto this Christmas-light-
lit porch where you'd rollick over a slurred sea

of neon lighters firing up enough 305s to drown a toddler
in smoke. Goddamn if that ain't exactly

what Tammi Miami (named on account cause
*sure as brimstone and shitfire* if she ain't escaping

to the Magic City real soon). Goddamn if she isn't
slowroasting her unborn son—of a shotgun

wedding in that crockpot cradled
beneath crossed arms. "Tam, you s-shouldn't

s-s-shouldn't," Tyler taps his nose. Damn if he doesn't
got more ticks than a mid-summer's deer carcass.

"Shouldn't what, Slick?" True, Tammi likes him
well enough but damn if her gaze ain't tempered glass.

Tyler leaning, right peach-pleased & dragging deep
he flicks the soggy slug of cigarette grassward:

"Ta-am, you shouldn't wear a b-bandana as a shirt." She flips
Tyler the middle acrylic, ruby as her ruddy bandana top.

Damn if them nights weren't a flurry of schwagy shooting
stars across the warped wood of a thousand porch boughs.

& how we howled: pack of coyotes circling an absent moon. Feeling
we'd bent the bars of its orange irons & finally, basking in the light.

# Teach Me How to Deregulate Rage

My mother laughs at my halfcocked jokes but that's about it—
a woman you'd see out in a bar on her first date
in months never knowing she's framing your arm
as a lever your fingers switches your whole
body a machine she wants to sledgehammer
hard until the knobs bust off and confetti filings
silver the barroom ceiling—her collar is so blue
it's made of skinned bluebirds plucked then shatter-fucked
china bluebirds—what an inadequate set of metaphors—she
is what thirty years wheelbarrowing through factories
does to some—what America's parody of Foxconn does
to most and mostly in hollers and dens and caves and small
towns that couldn't feel farther from a skyscraper with a king's
name embroidered orange at the top—she says she never liked
the name Joe Sixpack because she's never known
a Joe who stopped at six and everyone she really "knows
knows" buys Yuengling in bulk but it doesn't gush
through streets so much as gurgle down polyped throats
too tired to pitch yet another metaphor about their lungs
crinkling like two mercury–lined biohazard bags—a carnival
barker should walk just in front of my mother spinning
his black top hat—shake the dust around its rim and sing
to every passerby *look look* into its true dark its hollow—arsenic
beryllium cadmium chromium lead—then they might think
they've found a pot of precious metals—until the telos
of cancer climbs into the wombs of their lymph nodes—or rally
the congressmen at least—parade Capitol Hill—parade
them into the barker's magic hat—the ones who let the smoke keep
smoking the spoiled fish spoiling and babies tenderizing
in real wombs—cough out every metaphor for remission

because my mother can't hold down a conversation
without pieces of lung landing in her coffee or yet another
handkerchief mapping an undiscovered universe of silver
and stars of hard steel—find someone who will stay
hard as our erection around wealth creation who won't mix
their metaphors or turn heel but instead will show their metal
when standing witness as my mother is spilled out across another
hospital gurney bobbing as her barrel leaks silently down river.

# 0 to 60—One Horse in a Field

The engine of our silver 1984
Ford Bronco whirrs in a blue
night detour while my father whips
through a cornfield of husk
and copper seed pelting our windshield,
our clattering dash.

       "A shortcut," my father
       sings with Leonard Cohen.

              His boot double-times the pedal. Baby
              cousin Nora sleeps slouched against my lap.
              The ricketing cradles her. The tires lick up
              Mississippi Plain's dirt, dark and slurred
       at the edges of our car in brown bully splotches.
       I envy her unawares—to her new father's
       galloping hunt for newness toward land
       of enchantment: New Mexico.

       "Dance me to the end
       of love," he hambones
       against the steering wheel.
       I smell his scalding

              breath. I tell myself, don't cry out in fear. Don't
              wake
                Nora to this booze-saddled waltz of blue night
                pushing down plains, ripping up some unknown
                farmer's blackgold stalk and labor.

Crop parts in yellow waves,
and peaking through the treadless tires
of my eyes it's

    all
    open field
    sixty—or 60,000—
    horses running through unbound plain
    stampeding around our little silver car

        a streak, a tribe, a falling rock, an earth
        of muscled, shuddering
        hoofbeats louder
        than our radiator's rat-tat,
        and with my voice, I crack
        and stutter, "Stop."

We careen so close to a stallion,
that our bucking wheels are nothing
but a child's spinning top
below the bass of his thumping weight.

        Nora sleeps. And I won't wake
        her to this dream, wilder still.

Mare feet clomp and catch
    against our fender denting
its metallic smirk.

        Moon flecks sparkle in my father's
        good eye—the bad eye twists
        blue.

A tumult of flanks romp in dirty-
     skirted cream.     Horses
toward the edge of dissolving night.

              Red circles around their eyes,
                   their nostrils, their speared knees,
                       vessels of war
                indifferent to our bucking,
             our little—

I want to go where they're headed:
galloping into a different kind
of new, but I'm too afraid to ask.

            Take me anywhere
            except the land of enchantment:
            anywhere except New Mexico.

At my barefooted trembling, Wild
Buffalo and a sawed-off scuffle,
where Nora's dreams of feeding
wild ponies haven't yet caught
up to my father and his Wild
Hunt.

# Escaping Carlisle Indian Industrial School

*for an American Grandfather: "Robert L. Smith"*
*(Grandpaw Choo-Choo)*

"Min-ni-wa-ka!
Ka-wa-wi! Woop
her up! Woop her
up! Who are we?
Carlisle! Carlisle!
Ca-a-a-rlisle!" They cut
your black hair. Cut
the true name
out your raven's
tongue, *something*
*like Lonely Stars*?
You said, they cut
the herniated medicine
bag out the small
of your back. Cut
their new boy
into trapezoids,
kept you inside
grammars
of white, by
man's order.
You grew sick
inside your turtle shell
shoes, sick of cobbling
the hard-souled
moccasins of
gentlemen's feet
into something

even harder than a heel.
& then you jumped
rails, bare-feet first.
Said you had a yen
for wandering
& lantern-lit trains
where "Boxcar Bulls"
patrolled. *But no Christian*
*could catch me*, the best
part, you said
was knowing
you could match
the speed of any
freed train, any
tribe of iron horses.

## Tadodaho, Keeper of the People's History,
## of the Council Fire

Having escaped the reservation? in a hotel
along I-95, traveling with my dead Father's
ashes on the mantle or in a drawer or now on the dash,
I remember him asleep on the couch, he black bear
snores beneath my hands as I knead the dough
of his back, always waiting till the roar is loud enough
so I can stop trying to right the seven crooks in his spine.

We start up again beneath the frenzied hum of sodium vapor
streetlamps. Pitched into shadowed cheekbones, we
wait, licking shovel-shaped incisors "pancakes
or hot dogs?" he asks, and when I throw up
my voice for pancakes, a handful of flies startle
on the IHOP's enflamed LED display.

We stop for cigarettes tax-free twenty-four hours a day
and slip off the NY-11A on our way to West Virginia,
cricketing through mottled towns ashamed
of my growing pubic hair. Misshapen and monstrous
next to him in a dozen inns,
I whisper "can we find a new tribe?"
He says there will be Walmarts.
These are just as faithful.

Then, the word
'E x i l e' meant nothing but crackled
like birds hewn by Animikii's
finger from the sky.

I do not hear my father now in the wind between
rotten fences and blue dude ranch doors, but I mistook
a weathered jacket caught on a resting sledgehammer
for his broad silhouette before going inside.
Today, Yuengling and denim demons the both of us.

# Redeployment: Operation Noble Eagle, 14 September 2001—Present

*More than a politician's statistic*

Dear Jackson,

Remember spring. When for your Eagle Scout Project we built bird house / mansions. About twenty-eight of them. Four-storied with tiny foyers, even family / rooms: only, you told me they felt larger / than the peopled one / you were about to leave behind.

Remember summer. As we painted cedar / block after block a dark garnet. You finally hung / each grandiose house from hooks, or maybe we power-drilled them into the sides / of sycamores. I don't remember anymore. But I can still see us hanging hammers / in our carpenter jeans, imitating / chickadee songs. The tips of nails spearing / sunlight between our teeth. Really believing / we weren't just boy / scouts, but men.

Remember fall. From either Baglan or Khost or Saladin (it's hard remembering), / when you returned home with a garnet-colored / keystone tattooed on your shoulder. And I asked if you really missed / us: this old Pennsyltucky, our keystone state. You said, no. The block of red ink was a crest / for the buckets of your brother's blood poured out over Afghani sands: "The Bloody Buckets" "The 228th Iron / Soldiers." So, I started up the family truck and we headed for the bottom / of Penn Hills.

Remember winter. It was important / I go too, you said, *I got to*. I still don't / know why / we disassembled / each long-spoiled / birdhouse after birdhouse, piled the dark / planks of dead / wood high as our silver belt buckles. I crouched with flint and steel like the old / times, but you snuffed the cherry / end of your cigarette into the ball of our collective /

pocket lint. For awhile it burned, crackling. A collapsed / chickadee song.
I said maybe we should head back home / not inhale paint fumes. But,
you said the tumbled colors reminded you of yellowcake / uranium. Or,
maybe you didn't answer me at all. And for awhile we stood / together,
staring into the cracking / keystone of our last summer as scouts, / boys.

# Holler.

You & me's grandaddies churn to oil in cheap caskets: they're white-hot pollution, these corpses clogging every artery of our collective water body. It begins with the Susquehanna River, steamed cow patties stuck between their toes, tonight our kinfolk closed-canoe chase us boys, above ground—their flock of only begotten son's sons—toward the ass-end of this Lakawanna crick. Night's for bike racing and vandalism. So us boys don't speak of what's dead, Max's granpappy, poking holes in his leaky roof of tomb—how he snuffed himself a week or so back. (They say, his fingernails have already grown four foot, or longer than a wheel of fresh cheese.) Or Chuck's paw who died with rigor mortis in his cock. (Four foot, erect, we squealed something louder than a butcher's floor of stuck pigs.) Your own blood even made the rounds. What an ancient bastard, submerged downriver in a half-vacant double-wide, his coffin twice the size of your own trailer: truck: lean-to. (Granny refused being buried beside him—said sure as a cocked shotgun he's still grinding up the crabapple mash of his catcalling gums). You've outrun them. You got one perfect set of teeth between yins & you're all lubricated nutty with bolted on smiles, you're riding every other breath visible on each other's bike pegs, chromatic, downhill, helmetless, & airbound toward that night's rumored construction site. Behind, City Island is a great plain of obliterating peach orchards, lit up brighter than the ends of your stolen Swisher Sweets. You're high riding the hills of a scoliosed dragon's spine, spray paint cans clattering in backpacks. & already poor Cortel catches the bad side of a gravel trap, sprawling. You howl: *get up you fucking pussy*, laughing your asses

warm against dewy seats, but he has the good
shwag. So you dust off his pack & all take turns
flicking the shared lighter like old pros, inhaling
coughing, whooping like it isn't always the same damn weekend.
Whooping louder than any bleeding belt
burn you'll earn from getting home
late. Whooping like there really is construction in this town,
& a site to tag, & 16oz hammers for your carpenter jeans.
Whooping like you aren't the chased runoff of this burg's
miners & mill men & masons. Your white
tees stained with America's flag sputtering
against the beating coffins of your ribcages:
tees reading BUD LIGHT: KING OF
BEERS as the wind picks up
your spirits with mother's hands
& you give up
the chase at the edge
of the ass-end
of Conodoguinet crick.
You circle up:
each boy strangling the amber neck
of empty beer bottles.
& no one here knows
how to play
the violin, the horn,
or even a jerry-rigged guitar.
So. You stomp.
You clap.
You folk. Against
your father's
quiet desperation.
& the night resets again,
dissolving

the shoes
right off
    your feet.
    & and you slide
        into that crick
        headfirst. & for the first
            time
            today, really smiling.

# Warrior of The Rising Sun (1893–1959)

"Husband, soldiers are at the front,
hurry out the back," says
your wife not knowing men lie
in wait for you there also,

五  clover-clad men with their ghosts

go  bound to copper-handled katana,
the chevrons of their boot heels
freshly dug in your garden,
pointing like arrows toward
your three children, your home.

She hands you your best white
starched shirt and kisses your cheek
(this last part, the kiss, I only now imagine)

四  and as you go out the back, slipping

shi  on the shirt, they knock—knock
not at your door, but knock you
unconscious with the hip of a rifle, cut
from the big bones of a urushi tree
(this part, for sure, I know).

When you finally return home,
wading through an ocean of trees, after

三  forty days and forty nights, your white

san  shirt blooms red as ink ground
from a starbursting maple in fresh spring
as if your unstitched body was itself a battle map.

Now I call your daughter "Grandma
Zoomy," because Matsume is too hard

for a child to sound out. I rock on the yellow
carpet, sitting on her red painted toes
and ask, "Why

did they want grandpa?"
Because he wrote
a poem, something like a song, she
says. And I nod my head,
because I know lots of songs.
二 "What song though?" I say.
ni She says a song called See
The Warhorse Cry. I know
about horses, so I nod again
and say, "What's it about?"
About not going to war,
she says. And I nod
one last time, because I know
enough not to ask anymore
about war.

一 *See the warhorse cry.*
*Japan setting in the sun*
ichi *of his tear-stained eyes.*

40

# Obon, Festival of the Dead

*Generation I. Executive Order 9066*

Pursued by an ever-tightening net, my ancestral fish, twenty-something,
singing *Red Shoes, Red Shoes,* a children's nursery rhyme:
　　"Aka—i—kutsu—ha—ite—a,"
　　(A young girl wearing red shoes
　　has gone to America with a foreigner.)
　　"Only American songs," her husband says.
　　"A—E—I—O—U," she works over a cluster of vowels,
whispering to the infant girl on her back
while they wade Somerset,
toward Pennsylvania.


No one wants to travel back across a country, yellow-brown despairing,
full moon maples rollicking against pebble-pocked shores, my family
unharbored and demoored, San Diego wasn't its imagined paradise
in 1942 and fleeing. My grandmother escaping
the sea, carmine
　　　　sandals called
　　　　geta soaking in a blazing rain, birdsong lost,
　　　　having so
　　　　recently exchanged
　　　　surnames
　　　　　　　　*Hasebe* for *Smith,*
　　　　　　　　an island of motherless dark,
　　　　　　　　clothed by shorelines the color of waves.


*Nisei, Generation II. My mother*

(the infant girl) sings Momotaroson
to me (in a yellow house that smells like red

Marlboros and burnt ramen) of a little boy born
in the center of a softball-sized peachling, a stray
piichi that came bumping down a stream
like a present. She sings wholly
gaijin, my grandmother so proud
of her daughter's Japanese-less-ness.
We are all proud to celebrate my third
birthday at the Hibachi Grill: fire excising
from the throat of an onion volcano. Three
generations gather around to teach me
how to pick kernels of "gohan, gohan, go-han" up
off the face of a melamine plate.

*Sansei, Generation III. Alone*

I am returning to Japan-
town, decades later,
on an LA late summer
night on the corner of Rose
Street and 1st. Stretched ladders
of generations crowd
for the festival: lit-up
kabuki roam the streets
between rows of marinated
salmon, baskets piled
high with tiny,
dry sardines, niboshi
and sashimi sliced
onionskin thin.
Mochi flour
litters the air
as I pay beneath
amber paper lantern light

to have another brittle
box of Kitsune Udon
shipped
back to Pennsylvania.

I turn the corner, and
in a sake bar a white-face
woman stands on stage in red geta,
singing:
"Aka—i—kutsu—ha—ite—a,"
and for the first time it's only
the English I hear:

> "A young girl wearing red shoes
> has gone to America with a foreigner
>
> She took a ship from the wharf in Yokohama,
> Gone to America with a foreigner.
>
> Now her eyes have turned blue, I wonder
> about her as a foreigner in that country.
>
> Every time I see red shoes, I think of her.
> Every time I meet a foreigner, I think of her."

I wonder about her, now, as a foreigner
in my country. Widowed images
I cannot shake.

# Godzilla! vs. Six Links Trailer Park, an Unending Series of Tanka

I.
Clint Burkhart is King
of Monsters when he says I
ain't birthed by no paw,
but Taro(t)-dactyl: my wings
Steeler(s)-yellow Jap-girl, rat-girl thin.

I.




II.
Bust out fists, deep fry
him with the Atomic Ray:
yeller of a left hook.
We flint-to-steel fall. Chiming,
our arms groan heavy with rain-

I.




II.




III.
water falling, fat
as this Park's pleather bingo seats.
*Finish it chink,*
our ears ringing *ching, ching,* turn
your face & we fall forever—

## Beneath Carnival Lights

You can't stop morning
from melting plastic bags.

100 other goldfish twisty-tied
up and dreading a hot sunrise.

You're in mourning together
for the old 20+ gallon tank.

For the familiarity of the green leaf
that released you from an orange egg sack.

How'd you find yourself
in one of these again?

You are a woman now
but you have always had scales.

Bulging eyes, torn fins, and a fading
coat, you don't like what you see.

You've been told
you will be born

again and when
it's all over.

You like it when the man yells, *close
but no cigar.*

They say hope is his finger
poking the edge of your new egg sack.

You like it at night, when the coiled scales
glistening with light flicker on/off on/off.

You have ears for children's song.
Their blown bubbles remind you of home.

You think you are strong enough
to die in a toilet bowl.

# Our Last WWF SummerSlam

It's SummerSlam 1993 and my five
foot o bāchan, little Grandma Zoomy, wails
the sumo's moniker "Yokozuna! Yokozune!"
at the pineapple TV, at the top of her
lung (the other at the bottom of a hospital
biohazard bag, melted orange) she wails
atop the brown couch leather, melted
brown as her skin, both folded inward, paling
like the nasal tubes knotted around her knees, bent
cannula whining soft names of oxygen
down her throat: she translates for me as the man
with a microphone sings the Japanese national anthem,
"introducing the 6'6" 6-hundred pound Nippon phenom":

> *May your reign*
> *continue for a thousand,*
> *eight thousand generations,*
> *until the pebbles*
> *grow into boulders*
> *lush with moss.*

But the emperor is dead and now there is the World
Wrestling Federation, and while he sings, grandma
boos as Randy Savage interrupts and Macho
Man himself introduces Lex Luger in American
flag underpants. Cheer for your
family, she says, pointing to the blonde stranger
on screen, "always cheer for family."
We were alone together
in the apartment, alone in Somerset,
Pennsylvania, and how I wanted to cheer
beneath her heavy accent

for Japan while I massaged
the lip of her ashtray with a thumb.
Later I found out Yokozuna
was Samoan, born in Hawaii.
He didn't even speak
Japanese.

# The Down Syndrome Brother

Timiko, you are twenty-one & my mother bathes you
in my tub, while I watch from a crack in the door.

She scrubs around your penis, massages the centipede
scar in the middle of your chest: you were born

with a heart two sizes too small, with a penny-
sized hole at its core, I was told. Pink bubbles sudding

around your ears, my mother sings Japanese, always
Japanese. Clusters of sounds I can't yet pronounce. Clippings

of your toenails crescent the sink, she kisses your hairy
knuckles, dries you with a towel, helps you put on underwear.

Do you know you are her only brother? My oldest friend,
you try & Sharpie; your name in unending black sidewinders

over everything, as if Hershey Park is only a loping snake stain away.
I cannot teach you. To palm a name. Though I've pressed my lined

construction paper into your palms, again &. Like an abrupt,
wet blessing you circle a kiss onto my mother's forehead, both

dripping wet. *His handicap is Severe. S E V E R E.* A name
I've never quite palmed. "Like scissors without the safety?" A word

I'll never run with. *Balloons bobbing in a thunderstorm, lashed
around your wrist.* I groan like lightning, taller than the soft trunk

of you. Big brown dog of a suitcase at your Velcro shoes.
Headed for a government home. Because I am still just a child,

learning what it means to take care of myself. & you are thirty-one.
& our mother cannot stop palming old names for herself in loping

sidewinders: its creamy characters, O sweet cherry of liquid relief
& its release of red velvet dribbling down the split corners

of our mouths, family names we have yet to swallow. The name
of captivity alighting, its unfurled grey tongue: a swallow.

# At the End of My Street Corner: Jamaica, Queens

Young light
skin Native,
I wanted to hang
round n strut round
Jamaica, Queen's
rounded belly black
much the same
way white boys
just don't.

Wanted to be more
than Plexiglas
bystander round
Bernice's Studio—
(of) Dance
much the same
way straight boys,
those without
fifty cents
worth of class,
just don't.

Wanted to eat
Italian, Hillside
Cara Mia: *Beautiful
Darling* twirl n
roll round some blonde
angel's hair
cross my knuckles
much the same
way breathless boys

living four-fingered
all hand to mouth
just don't.

Wanted to fly
round feather-skinned
much the same
way fat boys
donut-holed up
under Queensbridge
just don't.

Wanted to fade
bullets tap tap-
dancing
round 109th Ave's
asphalt roof
much the same
way young blood
in this borough
just don't.

Wanted to trade
the bent branch
of my birth
name, whittle
its shape
into any thing
sharper,
less round,
streets smarter—
same way my Queens
traded

her Algonquin name:
Jameco *Beaver*
for
Jamaica *Rich*
traded the roundness
of a glass bead,
broke herself
damn near
sharper
sharper
than the end
of a spear.

# for a good boy we'll break all the rules

<u>Rule #3 "Start as Close to the Beginning as Possible"</u>
1945. *We must make room*
*for emptier bellies*, says the emperor.
They were eaten, pelts
fashioned like rabbits
fur for warmth. Akita Inu,
the national dog of Japan,
culled six hounds from extinction,
when grandmother was just
a little shojo. She freed her first
boy(-she-will-not-name)
into strangling kudzu, but he came back
again & again. Until her father begged
their neighbor to shoot this good
boy, because they had no
bullets & the spine of a sword
inherited is for man's neck not animal
hide. Because the emperor
is the entire nation, even if
its people had become a nation of dogs.

<u>Rule #4 "Be sentimental"</u>
Our fairybook beast, true hunter of a father held
your fifty-five-pound corpse
aloft by a single fist. Your hind
legs limp & stretched, you hung
like so many suppered
rabbits I'd imagined he & his fathers
had fired on a spit. But you were more than
domesticated, you were domicile. Earlier,
I carried your heavy

death from the Honda Civic
to the vet's dim bier. I carried your heavy
death from the final window-rolled car ride,
& into the garage, where we wiped
shit from your fur & wrapped you
in your old blanket: like the only burrito
that can make a man cry.
I know only you would forgive
me lines like that in a poem that stick
out awkwardly—
my lower back throbbed uncontrollably
when I dug your grave,
but for the heart of our mother
I had to have a sharper spine.


Rule #1 "Tell, Don't Show"
On her phone, our mother still
watches videos of your pained
breathing to remind herself
why she finally agreed.
*There's a difference between telling
yourself the truth & showing
yourself the truth*, she says.


Rule #2 "Write What You Don't Know, Always in 2's & 4's"
I know the ending
is the most important part,
but I don't know why
I placed the gifted mold
of your velvet paw & metacarpal
in my basement desk drawer.
Beneath the ground, damp,
& out of sight, maybe I hoped

it would grow again,
unlike you, into something
less final. Like a seed.
I would embrace any Act III
rebirth cliché.
For you,
I'd break
all the rules:

*For a Good Boy.*

# Misogi, the Patterned Act of Repenting

*My mother, she told me*      *to bury him deep,*      *the old bald-headed Chinese.*

*So, I buried him deep*      *& he stuck up his feet,*      *the old bald-headed Chinese.*

After so many recitations,      I too can see      the little boy hovering

over my mother's      school desk      so much emphasis

on his blondness      a belt      of freckles curling his mouth

as if simply singing      could straighten      the crook of his grin.

The teacher      the elementary teacher      instructs, *louder! louder!*

The worst part,      worse      than public humiliation,

was the crook      of a teacher's      grin, my mother says.

But now she rests      & we are two      grins,

sitting      crisscross-apple-sauce      atop a hospital gurney.

Treatment, she says      has finally made her      old, the bald-headed Chinese.

No longer laughing,      she has a wish      that I would stop shaving

my head as if I were      repentant      or in mourning. I remind her

we are not in Japan      & what's more      of my patterned baldness, surely the pattern is not     far away.          Nurses orbit

the bed,                      the stars          of our twin baldness.

My mother places             the plucked swans   of her palms atop my head:


"piichi fuzz" she says       "let it grow, swing  like gates around your eyes."

& I see                      her                 now beneath

her final                    wig's undoing       there is no future stubble.


Wind cracks                  the back            of my childhood

home,                        finally stumbling   through the front

door,                        corners of diagrammatic   crown mold.


A pattern:                   my daughter         she lies on the floor

swinging                     her tiny feet       back and forth,

shooing                      the bangs           from her eyes.

# notes grandpa gave the search party upon his rescue

in the woods i met a lady in a black dress

    or was it a dark tarp laid over sickled branches

    &

on the forest floor i coddled a mother rabbit nursing

    or was it a cracked violin uncased

        in my first year of sputtering faucets

i climbed a ladder of arms and wore a meaty necklace of sapphires

    it was hard fitting a family of bluebirds over my head

    &

when they crowned me king my subjects brought me gold bowls of
grape salad

    beetle feet tickled my tongue from my uvula insects hung

        in my second year of burnt stove smells

i was asleep in lavender cotton and a trickling of fairies came dancing
light

    hello, i'm cold and i think i'll go home now i said

    &

to the men in orange vests flashlighting

    or was it to the lightningstruck torch of an upright log

      in the third year of fire alarms beeping

they said they found me rolling like a dog in a dead thing

    i said please mind please mind the rabbits making rice cakes
        on the moon

    &

weeks later they found me again    dancing horizontal on the forest floor

    in the final year of my kettle's eternal whistling

# A Haibun to Define Kintsukuroi

*after Isamu Noguchi*

*The medium which is the earth itself has its own way—*
*and the fires of the kiln burn away my petty prides.*
    —from "Death (Lynched Figure)"

(n.)(v.phr.)
"to repair with gold"; the art
of repairing

The much-loved bowl sat up on a stool by the door all day. A very old bowl, his lips cracked, his brown bottom flattened, no longer was his basin ribbed and glistening like the other bowls. He did not smell as good as the tobacco bowl, billow like the thick kettle bowl, or sing with the baritone purr of the suribachi bowl (while tickled by a pestle); but when the potter came home she would say, "Hello my old bowl"; and the joy in the potter's voice would lift the edges of the much-loved bowl; and the potter would take off the heavy seal from around her finger and place it inside the old bowl. Then the potter would put her smooth hands—the cracks filled with dry clay—against the bowl's head and say, "Thank you for protecting my sigil, much-loved bowl."

pottery with gold
or silver lacquer and
understanding that

One night when the much-loved bowl sat restless atop his perch with the potter's ring snug inside his basin, he looked down at the moonlight writhing inside the newly lacquered bowls, still hot from the kiln, faintly aglow, and he stood at attention—unhappy. Honeycombed red and fractaled in stenciled blues, they lounged curved, tall, and the old bowl wanted to know how they made themselves so. So, he rocked himself to the stool's edge.

> the piece is more
> beautiful for being
> broken.

Before dawn, the potter woke and hurried to her work. "I knew you weren't finished yet," she touched the old bowl, dashed to pieces on the floor. And, shard by shard, she brought her much-loved bowl first that morning to the table, to lacquer it with gold; and she laid her sigil again into the old bowl's heart.

# Selling Cigars on a Coral Gables Corner 1987

Small lamb rack
    boy of my body
ma hung the color
of that coneflower
dress     right
off the scrag end of me

with her big paws
grin-shined up the length
of me     scraped
my baa baa black hair
back into tail
taut as a timpani

    drum

*Now grind it all the way*
    *to the bone* says my mama

say yes sir no sir mind
your ma'ams ma'am mind
your mammaries    pitch

a sale like it's a pole
like you got some slick
bitch's lemonade stand
squirt and competition in your eyes

wring out your lips
shout your tongue stiff

says spin six tables     shake
all comers     bleat for bill
after bleating bill     come
you prickled urchin
holler between pickings
pickle apart sweetbread streets
until the moon cries fat and then

say     *woman* say     *man* say     *sell*
you this whole stock
     the whole reeking lot

slurp the marrow     then strut
bang the stewpot     now swag

teetotalers gonna totter
at your feet

     tell them you baa
for a dollar if they don't
want none     crawl

across coffee dripped
sidewalks     sashimi
your elbows and knees

     baa for a dollar if they
want some shuffle up
and stuff it raw     meet deep
knock your elbows

notch your knees.

Now baa girl

Now sprint girl

sprint far away
now *grind*.

# Into the Red Devil's Horn

of a duct tape-wrapped microphone
the lead singer unbuckles
his diaphragmic roar:

*All you Hot Topic tourists*
*need to shove the fuck out!*
Anticipation fishhooks our assholes,

the drummer windmilling both sticks
she puts her whole sole into
the double bass pedal & stutter test.

The jaw of the dancefloor unclenches—
soapstone griddle of ceiling's drip
& rattle, our knee after knee bent

back in longing for the two-step
snap & moan louder than our father's
whip—sound is a torrent.

Water over umbrella-blossomed faces. We
puncture seams in the canvas
of each other's torsoed clap

& spilling. Horizontal
across this venue's meridian, faster
than a birdfeeder cage aswirl,

storm-caught. We spin-kick, we thrash,
we do a move called *Eating*
*The Dead*, while flatbrim hats shouting

B R U T A L on their underbellies
litter our banging head's thwack & we're a grin.
    Around every riff firing

brighter than the day
        our Lemoyne Dairy Queen burned
up. We are long boned & steel rakes upended—

        two-stepping over every tortured hour,
shedding the Saran Wrap around our mind's
        buffet of waking remainders, we mosh

it all out becoming mountains of upside
        down pelvic girdles,
collective, we are an excess

        of thrown elbows & the tattoos
that tourniquet our forearms,
        fists outstretched as if in want

for a blessing from the ram skull
        anthem. We call it deathcore.
Grindcore. We thirst for the rot

        of sampled screams. & soft mouths
spearing hard realities.
        We think we are the ballad

of the loner. In this song
        we are tapping the untapped.
With the last symbols crash

      we think we will finally vocalize
desire: the howl
      of microphone held too close

to speaker, reverb
      finding its way toward
a measure of rest.

# Contagion

they say   the yawn   is
contagious   the same
way   projectile
vomiting   can be
or we   wish   a smile
simply   were   or we're
thankful   sympathetic
farting   isn't   can you
imagine   the way
we claim   faith just   is
the way   hate leaps
from body   to
corpse   butter
knifes its   jam
thicker than   any
collective   yawn
understands   the way
our hands   itch
until   the auditorium
is a conversation   of cracking
knuckles   all   of   us
anticipating
a fight   that   is
just   around the
final   corner's
bend   as if
our temper's   pilot
light   reads   do not
ignite   but only   in
braille   wishing   we

knew a way    to clean
the skeletons
of our better    inventions.

# The Beginning of Science Fiction

This is fantasy, this is not our life.
We are not characters
who have yet to invade Mars,
who can stop their computers.
Now we are the gods who can unmake
the world in seven days.

The clock is handless.
Soon we will live forever
in heavy, stone bodies
with hieroglyphs stamped on our backs.
We speak words like overhead Muzak,
crackle and wire, deaf to trickling water.

The genre is alive. Invent something old.
Invent woman and man and trans
fully clothed in a garden;
invent an old man that will save the world,
a woman who carries her father
out of a burning city.
Invent a spool of thread
that leads a hero to destruction;
invent a continent on which he abandons
the man who saved his life,
with eternal insomnia over the betrayal.

Invent us as we are
how our bodies glitter
and we bleed out:
invent a shepherd girl who kills a dwarf,

a boy who grows in a giant tree,
a man who refuses to turn
his back on the past and is changed into pepper,
a girl who steals her sister's birthright
and becomes the head of a universe.

Unmetaphor every teardrop. Invent
chromatic love, painstaking innovation,
slow-spoken as a child's
index finger grazing that very first page.

# Light Escapes Us

In August 2028 the universe didn't bloom
     and shower us      with the spores of shared
consciousness. There was no      seventh sense
     needled on the upturned flypaper of our
eyelids,   no Great Awakening,       save our bodies,

how they shined.

Our no-seat-belt, face    -to-dash scars; our
teenage-gauged earlobes; our     sometimes     self-
inflicted knife-bite laced thighs; and our doctored-
up sun burnt skin  beamed,   slatted moon-
     light shuttling between swaying blinds.

Now NY, NY, is a Batman signal blinding;
the city is its own;  Northern Lights,
     spring from our fillings, from our sutured
hernia surgeries, our wholly
un    successful humpty dumpty   -ings.

We name our daughters Aurora, our sons
Borealis.  The street is full of charged particles,
waiting to be,     uncovered. Finally a reason
to put our sun glasses on   at night
while we weather the geomagnetic storm.

At the middle school game, when artificial
lights dim, the gym  nasium   ignites
in a disco ball tableau, exposing
     where soccer moms punctured basketball dads

with a wire hanger.     Where Nikko rescued
his keys from a toothy sewer drain, plunging
his heel through an exposed nail.
We roll down our sleeves,   (omitting
the lassoes), we adapt to the high-
-collared shadow of a dress shirt     (hiding
the halo), we trade our skirts at
Goodwill for jeans   (covering the razor-
nicked nightlights). It's a Sharia
renaissance in Times Square.

Some of us walk naked
like angels, luminously
undressed shooting
stars. But most, for fear
bundle up despite day's sun-
-leaked heat. Afraid
of anyone, ever getting
in, laid bare by the light—what
we're really made of.

# When One Has Lived a Long Time Alone

they are laserbathed and crystaleyed all of them
    candied bracelets circle upturned wrists
    in kneehigh neon socks they pitch their bodies
    forward an ocean wave of blood foaming
    against the stage's blackened shore
        everything is bright
        yellow
there is only the bass's bump her electric slap
    inside ear drums shorn
        the fragility of spilled tongues
    against one another molly roosts lip to lip
        to lip thin red butterfly bound
        by a current of light vibration
        limbs stretched piano wire tight
        to a vaulted ceiling's top
they call *bring out*
        *bring out*
    *The Beast*
        & i fear It
        will emerge
        as an empty room

           the absence of anything
           for light     to land on.

# Don't speak

*to strangers*, my mother
would repeat.

But the whole world
is a strangeness
replete.

& it speaks
to me. It speaks.

Mother Walks Free Despite Admitting Homicide
in Daughter's Death on Tribal Lands

*"No one speaks for that baby," said Bernadine Martin,*
*the Navajo Nation's chief prosecutor.*
        —Associated Press

What is the news?
        "Just put up a headline," says the editor,
        "no one will read it anyway."
        Reporters round the unresolved murders,
        as if the wind eroded every remainder.
                *There was swelling around the little girl's skull*
                *and hemorrhages around her brain.*

Who will count the bones?
        Silence pendulums over our
        brown body collective. We're told "Do not speak
        unless you are spoken" into—unless you are broken
        in two—unless
                *The scars on her 36-pound body were consistent with burns*
                *from a space heater, a curling iron and hot noodles.*

What does the eye witness?
        Maybe you see us windowed in another world.
        A dusty whirlwind shimmering through an Arizona night-
        watchman asleep, derelict-whipped, without a job.
                *There was a tear between her right ear and scalp.*

What is a hand?
        We file our nails into daggers. We sleep in each other's
        nail beds. We crack the wind's back and talk big

at the bar about pitchfork promenades. Imagining
our reflection in axe blades, when someone dear to us
　　says
　　　　*It's not enough to sing of cities sacked, of children*
　　　　*slain. What with Murder's maw splintering wide*
　　　　*all across our plain.*


　　　　Then


Who will speak?
　　Who will speak?
　　　　　*Who will speak?*

# Teach a Man Cruelty and He'll Never Forget Your Face

On my seventh
birthday
Grandpaw Caribou
cobbled me

a pair of deerskin
moccasins.
By the time
we got
to his best friend
Bob Birkhouse's
they was all but
beat to shit.

Bob, Paw said
had the face
of a river bed 'n
bred the best
dogs in Emporium.
Period.

I didn't ask how
but Paw took
my ears in his pocket
told me: Mr.
Birkhouse tied litter
after litter of pups
up in St. Mary's
Walmart trash
bags, wriggling

like fish
on the line.

Then he'd pitch 'em
over the rust-spackled
bridge until Gia
herself yellered
up the perfect pup
to raise.

Then he'd break
the dog
again & again

like so many sticks
of tinder I brought
silent to our fire
that night. Searing
into my eye's delicate
skin the face
of a river bed.

# So much depends

upon a mother opening        the door
her work        boots are just boots        but her soul
is dirt-caked  hair bunned        back so tight
her brow glints        brighter than steel

she clods across the kitchen floor
sole        heel        sole        heel        rhythmic mimesis
of the hydraulic press she's left behind        for now
her palms are finally warming        beneath the faucet's factory
of squeaky gush        I want to        hug her but the confetti
of metal filings shake        free        from her canvas pants

how to take        off overalls        let them slip
to the floor as if never to be brought back        to skin
let them lie vacant of meaning        an infinity symbol        legless
holes        don't concern yourself with theatre        you've never even
been        fiddle with the sterling buttons        scraping grime
out the filled dinner plates        of your crumbling nails        don't moan
as you unclasp the plastic bra hooks        for the sake
of your son        sitting on the floor don't        tell him easy
mac        is all there's for supper        wheelbarrow race
fear against insomnia        microwave all the possibilities
tell yourself you are rich in love        but know the price        of tender
meat

# Loss of a Man's Tail: Baring One Native Son Bald

*When the Indian is dying, tell me how to at least save the man.*

barring tails birds
could never fly.
fish could never
swim. the beaver
ever unbalanced.

Tail-torn, my new headdress
is an aureoling starfish, a white
plague circumferencing the old
blackberry bushel of my head.
Laurelling, illegitimate, bare
as my brown knees. All my hair
follicles lie dormant in their once wombs,
a cobwebby bier. Lice are starving. The comb
is crying, Gano'ha Earth's given up
her seeds. Now my only ritual
& morning rite is pressing clippers
close to my scalp. Mourning
my forefather's spirit fast fading
down the sink. I've given away
the rhinestone combs, the ornate turtle shell
beaks. Traded them for dreams
of drowning in foaming Rogaine & side effects
of swallowing tabloid tinctures,
shrinking my testicles useless as licorice jelly
beans. Maybe then my pores will overflow
with meaning, maybe then I'll plié
a pompadour, sprout a hearty

squashblossom like a brown-face Princess
Leia, let my tail curlicue in a chongo,
or at least roached up in a beetley black
top knot. What binds tighter than the knitter's hand
arrowing heads of lush crochet? What grows
fast enough to outpace the loom's
greased bough? In fistfuls
I will gather all the hair casketed purple
after long-dying & uncork myself, offer
the baled bougainvillea as a barker, "Here!"
I will ode, "is this harvest
enough to imitate the whitetail
deer, calm muddy waters, cascade
with the all fury of fertility
in a stallion's black mane?"

## Los Alamos, New Mexico: An Open Letter to Radiation Poisoning

It's 1943 & you're moaning your secret:
Manhattan Project. Ore, more accurately,
you're what our pickaxes tick-tick-scrape.
Shunting of our land, splintering Church Rock
& dethroning Crown Point. You're what
our native sons dig for: atomic #92.

It's 1945 & you're a rich tenor rising in fat men's
throats. You're the splintered soprano squealing
above Nippon sons, a hollow bullet served steamed
on "Silverplates," Boeing B-29 "Super-fortresses."
You're the loudest whistle whining above metropolitan
Japan. Where we hide beneath our desks. It doesn't
matter: you're so full of yourself since growing out
of nothing but the dry pustules shaved from our art-
eries, dug from the dirt of our burial mounded souls.
We built fire lines, then picked the petals off oleanders red
& pink: the first flower to bloom after your
kaboom at our scalded pink feet.

It's 2012 & you're *still* the abandoned Northeast Church
Rock mine. One of half a thousand permanent
waste sites oozing out of the Navajo Nation's
crippled left shoulder. You're not a secret
anymore, skittering down the runaway
veins of our once big men, our once little boys, the ones
with pickaxes who are like you now:
hollow & scraped & shunted
rising with atomic #redwhite&blue.

It's 2000-fill-in-the-blank & you're the only voice
left to make sure aspens bloom again in our spring:
so our boys can pick up axes
silvery-grey, soft and strong, good for pulping
the paper our children use for finger painting
forests of strawberry blonde.

# The Act of Soul Ferrying

Act I: Fall 2016, Waiting for the Chaplain

Adderall flicks a light switch
on inside your head. Meth
is the Sun. My brother told me
that once. Tells me nothing
now while he sleeps bound all the glory
found top a gurney. The slinky organ
of his ventilator struggles up
a fogged tube & back. He's
always been sickly. Self
inflicted mostly. Blame Quetzalcoatl
the soul-ferrying snake
god, he'd say through a smile.
No, this time everyone ate. Men,
gods, & crow. Meth had sucked
the length of his limbs. Teeth
starbursting gums in the back
of his head. A nailless naked toe
edging past sheets. This time
Quetzalcoatl found him
on his brown hands & shredded
red knees warming or waiting
on a sewer grate just outside the city.

*What? What are we*
*gonna do about your brother here?*
The doctor didn't bother
removing the nibbled Bic
from between her fingers
when offering me the fortune

creased on her open palm.

Act II: Summer 1998, Finding the Chaplain

Honest, I thought he was
a felled log so enormous yet
emaciated gray speckled with
life. Lying on his side & I
saw a width of branching
antlers scrape stone. Labored
breaths. Bats veered & crickets
wallered. Smaller wildlife waited
patiently from beside my little boots.
I undid my uniform, leaving
the khaki balled at my feet, standing
at the edge of water my bareness met
slush of river, blowing me cold
like I was a cup of hot soup.
When I reached shore, would he
speak to me? The voice
of an old god in my hands.
His eyes large as plates
of pitch & worming. Breathe
in &. Winedark spittle flung
nubs of teeth. Breathe out &. We
faded along side blue light's
loping night. & on my knees
I gripped his horns tighter
than stolen handlebars. I swear
I thought hard about things
whimpering on the edge. War
& pain & white hospitals. Marbles

of blood swam from his thighs: dimpled
red fish being birthed into river mouth
& I pressed his muzzle under. Tension
kicking and crippled hooves slid
further into silt & marl. Little life
splashing around us. Illuminated he
couldn't lift himself from the hammered
face of rock.

Act III: Spring 2017, Becoming the Chaplain

I stutter over every river
rock. Guiding his horns, gentle.
My breath sputters & ripples
of water blur around his brown
head. I feel deeper creatures
lurking where I cannot see.
Clouds pool and pillow like painted
sprites of past recollection.

After I am old & bent out of time
& all materials, the deer will be
reborn as some great warrior or so
I hope. & so I hope a man I love
will likewise be divided back
into his origins. I lie again small
& young next to my brother, we two
small-bodied specks amidst a great swell
of living afterbirth. His eyes like giant
plates of pitch. I feel the prickle
of his fur against my chest.

*What are we doing*
*about your brother here?* When
the doctor placed her open palm
on my shoulder I didn't bother
telling her about the deer & the river.
My brother slumped
beneath a sheet of white river cloth.
A felled log floating so
enormous emaciated & grey.

# Economy

Even though I'm told
death is a sunk cost
at the funeral,
I don't understand
the exchange rate.

Fleshy durables in the casket
have expired. The corpse
awfully well-dressed for
a brittle boat of unpaid
property tax.

Burn me. Pour me
as a final offering
to earth alive,
and now ashes. Never
a phoenix, still just
a dead thing.

Unconsciousness,
as if all my cents
will be sifted,
somewhere upon
a senseless death.
Then what will be
worse: embalming,
cremation, or lost
at the bottom
of drugstore Coinstar.

# Of Reach

That summer there was no cub left in me.
Gradually they took down the placards.
"Let her bars rust over," said the keeper all at once.

Between my rock and the sky, I was more
tiger than lion. Striped and yellowing,
canines broken over fat.

At night mothers purred out of the earth.
They still remind me I am never
more than in heat.

At daybreak I can see them cooling
their lithe anatomies poolside, eloping
so many babies between their hips.

What will I be
by the time they are also middle-aged?
I can't see past the edge of my cave.

If I tear the quick of my claw,
I want you caring. Enough to glue it.
Let me hold on awhile.

Don't lay me gently
on the veterinarian's floor,
but breathless in my final heat.

Fill me with the smell
of your mane. Nuzzle my jaws
till they are raw and I'm what's weeping.

Sink your paws into my spine.
Rupture my trachea's roar,
before it gives accord of its own.

Don't throw me to my own
kind. Of suffering, I've already
gorged. Fang whitener, tail lifter,

coat shiner, really I've tried.
To acquire a taste for all the offal.
Butcher man's throat O ever out of reach.

# "please take a seat, the doctor will see you shortly"

america lukewarm & turgid
on the local coroner's table
rigid as a wrecked school bus
so much yellow brown & black.

they prodded me along

i tucked a single finger up
under the botox lip
& pried george
washington's false
teeth apart with my thumbs

i considered my learning
about the heart

i scooped out america's
jack-o-lantern brains
i massaged its flagpole

i applied the silver
bell to its tongue

now they look at me
like a mission
to mars burning up
trust me i think i know
how hollow this examination
will prove

but someone gave me the bone saw so
here I am.

# I Am

I am the black      and white      and red all over S&M priestess
howling      like biblical Wisdom
for Solomon's sky-shattering      discernment from every street
corner. Peeling      apart this electronic newspaper      licking dark
wires fired      and my hair is kindling that I      break off to
ignite
our arguments that smell      so solipsistic      because I cannot
pluck off my nose      so you can smell      what I have smelled
or dip my kingfisher's beak      into the eyes of a thousand      lidless
little stories: goldfish      heads who have no voice      yet I know some
cry
for: "Tyrannicide!"      I get it. We're both      rocking      down the back
of every
blue donkey,      dancing down the trunk      of every claret-red
elephant,
sucking      the shaft of a thousand      golden trumpets, and was it
Uncle
Calvin who said that      on Jesus' thigh a name is      tattooed that no one
knows but Himself?
         Revelation I am.
Telling my children      about Rumpelstiltskin's scalp      bought and
sold
and thrown      from the spread corollas of      my finger tips so that the
child
on my lap can      imagine      what I used to, as I read to him even
if only
for a little while, for ahead there is grief      and great trials. He doesn't
need to know about      blood  swirling in a wine-dark scrim
shanked
from a fleeing Arab's side because for now      I am

the pink mist     sprayed on a table     collected   in pouches
methamphetamines
wailing to be   snorted so I can soar through your  lymph nodes and
remind
you that when you were six     years old there were only two
women you
loved your      mother and your mother and your mother—and—
my fear is
        not that I Am
failing at anything. but rather        succeeding
at those things      which don't really matter.

# Notes

*Thank you personally to each and every one of my students. Without you this collection would not have been written with such immediacy and love: connection to a beating heart.*

*Thank you: Lucia Maria Alvarez, Nia Byrd, Raina Coleman, Donald Foiani, Mariam Girgis, Emese Eva Hof, Junhe Huang, Tyler Kelly, Codi Lee, Jacob Madaus Brueck, Alvaro Mazaheri Sanchez, Natassia Tan Najman, Michael Nickolas, Darien Pereira, Connor Shatz, & Yan Xia.*

*Thank you: Claude Christopher Jr. Carpel, Brittany Chandani, Kathryn Cioffi, Kathryn Gonzalez, Joana Kemeny, Shane Malcolm, Andy Li, Brooks Peterson, Bobby Price, Anthony Pumilia, Manvi Rajan Seth, Jordan Shito, & Julia Weinman.*

*Thank you: Luciano Alfaro, Jessica Grenier, Gabriela Hernandez, Zhao Ma, Brooke McDermott, Quinn McKinnon, Lucia Pampana, Sam Schnur, Sakile Ayanna Simmons, & Gabriel Stephane Umbert.*

*Thank you: Frias Albar, Kelly Alworth, Divina Mohan Chandiramani Bellani, Zachary Currier-Martin, Solana Garcia Flores, Radhika Vivek Gore, Joshua Kaufman, Max Koncza-Oddone, Oliver Labrador, Pooja Patel, Joseph Ramus, Jordan Rezman, Paul Sigars, Victoria Steward, Ellie Stockinger, Channing Washlesky, Chensuzi Zhang, & Jing Zhu.*

*Thank you: Emma Avila, Dominique Bryan, Andre Carty, David Chung Mo, Facundo Ciano, Nicholas Coviello, Nicole Franco Averbach, Thomas Glasser, Juan Rafael Gomez, Travis Homer, Olivia Jacobi, Stuart Raty, Tony Roye, Alexa Skolnik, Tedral Smith, Michael Taylor, & Simon Young Un.*

*Thank you: Summer Atteya, John Tsenkoom Bawa-Shitgurum, Dayrelis Castillo, Grecialis Colon, Kendrick Criales, Marcus Cruz, Sherer Desinor, Eduarda Deziderio, Leonardo Diaz, Khaleb Fernandez, Melissa Flores, Alberto Fuentes, Alexa Marie Inda, Kesi Darnell Land, Javier Lopez, Luke Luria, Estela Mesa Armas, Marlon Navarro, Melissa Ortiz, & Giselle Sanchez.*

*Thank you: Anthony Balaguer, Emilio Bayona, Mateo Blanco, Isabel Burgos-Ekmejan, Nayvel Cairo, Dylan Casanova, Yolanda Correa, Molses Del Rio, Felipe Del Valle, Beatriz Doval, Sabrina Fernandez, Carlos Garcia, David Granizo, Franchezka Guzman, Jessica Hernandez, Gavin James, Tatiana Jimenez, Mikeala Maragh, Luis Elias Montablan, & Marbelis Rodriguez Borquez.*

*Thank you: Kaily Alvarez, Michel Lazaro Castro, Diana Castillo, Giovanni Chinea, Christian Alonso Duque, Francheska Espinal-Gomez, Yazmin Fuentes, Rolando Garcia, David Gonzalez, Gabriel Hernandez, Jasmin Johnson, Juanita Lopez Muriel, Janet Mejias, Kevin Morales, Andrea Pena, Brigitte Ramirez, Danile Reinbold, Christian Rodriguez, Rene Rodriguez, & Tristan Rodriguez.*

*Thank you: Vivian Batista, Olenia Caymares, Daniel Cotayo, Ashley Dennis, Barbara Gonzalez, Luis Gonzalez, Alfredo Melendez, Octavio Perez, Ryan Perozo, Victoria Valcarcel, Victoria Vargas, & Abigail Zuluaga.*

*Thank you: Erik Acosta, Dinora Aguila, Yousif Zaid, Agnelly Amador, Monica Arevalo, Paola Alejandra Ayala, Claudia Campuzano, Stephanie Cisne, Julio Colon, Natasha De La Rosa, Christian Fernandez, Sabrina Fernandez, Luis Gonzalez, Yanci Ainnee Gonzalez, David Granizo, Melanie Ibarria, Angieleen Juvert, Elizabeth Lemus, Anishka Morales, & Octavio Perez.*

*Thank you: Jumana Akbar, Muhanad Alenezi, Nawaf Almutairi, Venkat Nakuldev Reddy Basani, Dunya Bulut, Rebecca Dugini, Trevor Fellcetti, Lina Ferrari, Clarisa Ferre Vazquez Figueroa, Gustavo Gamboa Malaver, Amalia Ivaldi, Elizabeth King, Celine Mamedova, Filippa Moerk, Emily Orellana, Kimberly Patterson, Katrina Riveron, & Camila Rocha.*

*Thank you: Alexandra Chavez, Altadonna, Jinglin Chen, Tao Chen, Sofia Contreras Ojeda, Rachel Farmer, Bridget Gidlow, Stefani Gonzalez, Martin Haberer Sabah, Qiheng Jiang, Simon Lehrer, Elias Juan Diego Lugo-Fagundo, Syed Golam Mohaimen, Blake Nossel, Amber Ponder, Xinwen Wu, Jiamin Zhao, Nan Zhou, & Yijie Zhu.*

*Thank you: Joseph Bannister, Renee Booker, Sage Burch, Lyle Davis, Andrew Herrfurth, Andrew Kogut, Emily Parks, Rebekah Rashford, Patrick Reilly, Kara Rogers, Emory Russo, Bethany Skadin, Ryan Witkowski, Natalie Yelenik, & Emily Yu.*

*Thank you: Alice Ball, Rollie Beatty, Ryan Bernstein, Bryce Bush, Georgia Dettmann, Owen Dunn, henna Fraiman, Alex Hopson, Jordyn Jones, Daniel Lowenstein, Maya McKnight, Sean Mills, Fernando Quezado, Henry Rosenberg, Hannah Sawa, Aliya Shen, Zoe Stern, & Zachary Zhao.*

*Thank you: Meagan Barrett, Samantha Bass, Nadine Benavides, Joseph Bernstein, Talon Bevan, Cara Campbell, Justin Drew, Telvin Hotobah-During, Helen Lam, Morgan Mullings, Chizi Odidika, Olubusola Opensanmi, Steven Plovan, & Wanying Zhao.*

*Thank you: November Buchanan, Dierra Carter, Maxwell Costes, Mason Freeman, Grayson Hanes, Bowen Jiang, Sophia Keifer, Margot Kohler, Chelsea Kovinsky, Kendall Lambert, Anh Le, Michael Melvin, Jaz Quaranta, William Rende, Alexander Seibel, Max Sobkov, Sophia Stratakis, & Bryson Webb.*

CPSIA information can be obtained
at www.ICGtesting.com
Printed in the USA
BVHW03s2156081018
529656BV00001B/50/P